Just a Kentucky Boy

by

Chaplain Lieutenant Colonel Harold S. Johnson
United States Air Force Auxiliary

TEACH Services, Inc.
P U B L I S H I N G
www.TEACHServices.com

World rights reserved. This book or any portion thereof may not be copied or reproduced in any form or manner whatever, except as provided by law, without the written permission of the publisher, except by a reviewer who may quote brief passages in a review.

This book was written to provide truthful information in regard to the subject matter covered. The author assumes full responsibility for the accuracy of all facts and quotations as cited in this book. The opinions expressed in this book are the author's personal views and interpretation of the Bible, Spirit of Prophecy, and/or contemporary authors and do not necessarily reflect those of TEACH Services, Inc.

This book is sold with the understanding that the publisher is not engaged in giving spiritual, legal, medical, or other professional advice. If authoritative advice is needed, the reader should seek the counsel of a competent professional

Copyright © 2011 TEACH Services, Inc.
ISBN-13: 978-1-57258-655-0 (Paperback)
ISBN-13: 978-1-57258-656-7 (Hardback)
ISBN-13: 978-1-57258-657-4 (Ebook)
Library of Congress Control Number: 2011925339

Published by
TEACH Services, Inc.
www.TEACHServices.com

Just a Kentucky Boy is dedicated to my dear companion without whose assistance and insistence it would have never been written.

I would also like to thank the following for their assistance in proofreading, suggestions, and typing of the manuscript:

Vickie Boling
Margorita Maldonado
Doris Smith
Naomi Zalabak
Sunny K. Zengler

I also would like to dedicate it to my dear children and grandchildren:
Stephen, Lynda, and Ceilidh Johnson
Karen, Pat, John, and Marjorie Burns

Table of Contents

Chapter 1   Growing Up in the Bluegrass State 1

Chapter 2   Starting Out on My Own 11

Chapter 3   Military Life and the Army Band 13

Chapter 4   School, School, and More School 25

Chapter 5   From Georgia to the Middle East 30

Chapter 6   New Beginnings 42

Chapter 7   A Life of Service 53

Chapter 8   Overflowing Gratitude 56

Chapter 1

Growing Up in the Bluegrass State

Harold Stephens Johnson—just a Kentucky boy—was born on February 11, 1928, in Campbell County, Kentucky, to Loretta (Stephens) Johnson and Oren G. Johnson. I was that boy.

At the time of my birth, my father was working in Cincinnati, Ohio, and had rented a house just across the river in Newport, Kentucky, where I was born. Some time later my family moved to Tipprel, Tennessee, which no longer exists, but was just a short distance from where Daniel Boone is supposed to have entered Kentucky at Cumberland Gap, Tennessee.

My father worked as a finish carpenter, later working for the Doctor Evans Coal Mine near Middlesboro, Kentucky, a small mining town in Bell County at the foothills of the Cumberland Mountains. He was responsible for keeping the tipple in repair so the coal could be properly graded as it came from the mine. The coal was carried to the tipple where it was dumped into the bin, which had large metal grids with different-sized holes in it. As the coal traveled down the mountainside, it was graded by the metal grids, dropping into designated holding bins to be loaded for shipping.

At that time, all coal was mined by hand with no machines to dig or load. The coal was hauled out of the mines by a donkey pulling a car on the tracks. When they were close to the entrance of the mine,

Just a Kentucky Boy

the driver would stop and take the blindfold off of the left eye of the donkey and put it over the right eye. This was done so that the donkey's eyes would adjust to being in the mines or out in the bright light.

While living in Tipprel, Mother gave birth to my brother, Paul Martin, who lived for only a short time. I faintly remember Dad making a little casket for the baby and Mother lining the inside. He was buried in the little cemetery behind Lincoln Memorial University in Harrogate, Tennessee.

Shortly after my baby brother's death, my mother became very ill. While she was in the hospital, my older brother, John, and I stayed with some neighbors. The only thing I remember about that experience is that they took us snipe-hunting one night and scared us so badly that it was a long time before I overcame my fear of the dark. What made it even worse was that I had to walk over the same mountain each evening to meet their son, who was studying at Lincoln Memorial University in Harrogate. One of his legs was amputated, so I was responsible for helping him carry his books. The way the neighbors treated us made Dad so angry that he wanted to kill them. I'm glad he didn't.

It wasn't too long after that that my mother passed away and was buried in the same cemetery as my baby brother. I remember many times waking up in the night crying for her. I have only a few memories of my mother since I was so young when she passed away. I have searched for her grave several times, but cannot find it since no headstone was placed there. In addition, my mother's side of the family remains a mystery to

Loretta S. Johnson
Mother (Deceased)

me because I never met any of my relatives on her side. I do know that she was born in Cincinnati, Ohio, and that her family was of the Catholic faith, but that's about all I know.

With no mother at home, John and I did our best to help around the house while Dad was working. One summer we tried our hand at canning the blackberries we had picked. Somehow we got them mixed up with kerosene, which quickly ended our canning experience.

When we were not in school, John and I would go to work with Dad. We walked about seven or eight miles from our home to Dad's worksite near Middlesboro, Kentucky. Of course, we usually took a shortcut by walking through the tunnel that went through Cumberland Mountain. Dad knew the train schedule, so we would always go before it was time for the trains to run. The tunnel was about one-half mile long with a steep grade about halfway through.

When we came to the entrance of the tunnel, Dad would have us stop so that our eyes could adjust to the dark. He would then say, "Now, keep your eyes on the small light at the end of the tunnel, and stay in the middle of the track." As long as we looked straight ahead, all went well, but whenever we took our eyes off the light ahead, we would lose our footing and fall down. With all the smoke and soot left by the old steam trains, you can imagine what we looked like when we got outside again.

When school was in session, we attended a small four-room school in Arthur, Tennessee, about three miles from home. I remember that they gave us Postum to drink and a sandwich to eat for lunch. That is the first time I remember having mutton sandwiches. Later, we attended the one-room school in Tipprel, which was held in the Methodist Church and was closer to home.

Growing up in Tennessee, I always looked forward to the fall. After stripping and cutting the sorghum canes, we attended the community "stir off," as we called it. That was when the community got together to make sorghum molasses. This always took place during the full harvest moon. The men would squeeze the juice from the canes using an old turn mill drawn by a horse or a mule. The elderly ladies would sit by the pan, stirring the juice until it boiled down into molasses. When it was ready, the ladies would call, "Stir off." When we heard them call, all of us children who had been running and playing came running to the pan with our "spoons," which we made from the cane stalks. Each of us got to eat some of the foam. Whatever foam was not eaten was dumped into a pit. Invariably, before the night was over, someone would fall into the pit.

Music played an important role in our lives. During the evening, while the molasses was being made, there was a lot of good old mountain music and singing. Sometimes there was even square dancing. I remember, especially on Saturday nights, Dad would play the fiddle for square dances, as well as call them at times. If we were not attending a square dance, we would tune the radio to Renfro Valley, Kentucky, listening to "Renfro Valley Barn Dance," or else, we would listen to the "Grand Ole Opry" in Nashville, Tennessee. Saturday night was a time when we could stay up late because we didn't have to get up early on Sunday morning.

Guns were also a part of our lives, serving as protection and a way to obtain food. Dad was a real sharpshooter. Looking into the creek by our home in Tennessee, he could see a water snake and, standing on the porch, shoot it. He also used his gun for killing rabbits. One fun thing he would do with his shooting skills was to go into the mountains just before Christmas and shoot mistletoe out of the trees to bring home for Christmas decorations and to share with neighbors.

In addition to working in the mines, Dad took care of our plot of land. I always enjoyed going with Dad when he was plowing in the fields because he would let me ride Old Charlie, our horse. I fell asleep many times while riding, but I never remember falling off. When it came time to strip the corn, I remember working with Dad. Sometimes I would get into what we called "pack saddle" larvae, which gave a very wicked sting. There were usually several on a single corn blade, which made it hurt worse. As soon as I got stung, Dad, who chewed tobacco, would spit tobacco juice on my arm to deaden the sting. What a relief!

In addition to working the land, I always enjoyed helping Dad cut pulpwood with the old two-man crosscut saw. It was really hard work, but I especially enjoyed cutting trees down for firewood or building materials. When Dad built our new barn, we made all the shingles, splitting them one by one out of blocks of wood. The old barn was a sturdy building. One time when a tornado came through, the only damage to our place was the displacement of some of the corner logs of the barn.

Several years after Mother passed away, Dad met Rose Parker, and later they were married. This was his third wife—both my mother and his first wife had died. His first wife became very ill with pneumonia and passed away, leaving my father with four children to care for—two girls, Dorothy and Vera, and two boys, Robert and Lawrence. I do not recall ever having any contact with my grandparents on my father's side.

It was shortly after Dad married Rose that we moved from Tennessee to Middlesboro to be closer to Dad's work and cut down on the time he spent walking to his job. Dad had put our home up as guarantee that he would pay Mother's hospital bills. Since he was not able to meet the payments on time, the hospital took our home. However, Dad was able to rent a small house in Middlesboro. Later, after several moves, he was able to buy a place we could call our own.

Just a Kentucky Boy

It is interesting that all the places we lived in were close to a set of railroad tracks. Just a short distance from our home in Tipprel was a turntable. The engine would be put on it and turned around so that it would be heading back to Knoxville. Each day, about noon, the passenger train coming from Knoxville to Middlesboro would pass our place. We would stand on the back porch and wave to the engineer, Charlie Frailey. We had ridden his train many times and considered him our friend. Each day when we were there to wave to him, he would toss an apple or something else to us. Occasionally we had the privilege of riding in the engine with him, which was a great treat. The first time I rode in the engine the fireman asked me to step on a lever on the floor for him. When I did, you can imagine my surprise when the door to the firebox flew open and I saw flames leaping up and felt the heat pouring out! Since the old steam engines ran on coal and water, there was a place at Cumberland Gap just before the tunnel where they filled up with coal and water. We lived close to the yard where the empty coal cars and boxcars were parked. The boxcars were lined with brown paper, which we sometimes scrounged through to use for writing paper.

When we moved to Middlesboro, we were again close to a set of railroad tracks. Many times we would pick up coal that fell off the cars to use for our fuel. In addition to the coal, we obviously burned wood. At one time, the mountains were covered with chestnut trees, which had been killed by blight. The fires on the mountains had destroyed many of them, but we were able to find remains to take home for kindling to start fires. We also looked for pine knots from trees that had died to use to start fires.

On our little farm, we had chickens, hogs, and two cows, which John and I milked. We had all the meat we could eat. Every week we had chicken, at least on Sunday. Each year Dad killed two hogs,

Growing Up in the Bluegrass State

weighing around four or five hundred pounds. We had the slaughtered hogs and beef to eat. My stepmother made soap from the fat of the hogs. With two cows, we had all the milk we wanted. We also made our own butter and buttermilk. To churn butter, we used a half-gallon Mason canning jar as a churn. We shook the cream back and forth in the jar until the butter formed.

During those early years, our evening meal consisted of cornbread and buttermilk. For breakfasts, we usually had biscuits, eggs, and gravy. I grew up on biscuits, cornbread, oatmeal, beans, milk, eggs, and meat.

Living in a coal-mining town, we shopped at the commissary, the company store where miners could buy their food and household goods. Part of the miners pay was script or tokens the company issued for the people to buy things in the commissary. You could go to the commissary and ask for a pound of "miner strawberries," and they would give you a pound of pinto beans. One of my favorite meals was, and still is, a big bowl of beans and cornbread with a glass of buttermilk. As I mentioned before, we had plenty of meat to eat, which, at times, included rabbit, squirrel, and fish. We mainly caught catfish.

In the summer I would get up early and head for the blackberry patch. When it was light enough to see the ripe berries, I would begin picking. Usually, I was home by 7:30 or 8:00 a.m with my bucket full of berries. In addition to blackberries, we also picked huckleberries and strawberries. We would go into the mountains, camp out at night in an old abandoned log house, and be ready to pick wild berries just as soon as it was light enough. Mom would can all we needed. After that, I would pick and sell them for fifteen cents a gallon.

When we lived in Tennessee, we didn't have running water or inside plumbing. We had to carry our drinking water from the community water supply about a quarter of a mile from the house. Fortunately, we had a wooden barrel at the corner of the house to catch rainwater for washing clothes and taking baths. Using an old galvanized tub, we always had a full bath at least once a week. Being the youngest, I was the last to get my bath. One day Dad decided that we needed a new outhouse closer to the house. While digging the pit, he struck water. That pit became a well and the source of our water supply.

In the fall when we gathered the corn, we saved the shucks for making shuck beds for the winter. We shredded the corn shucks, and Mother cut the ends off and filled the ticks, which was the covering that was filled with the shucks. The shuck beds were very comfortable and warm. We cut enough corn to make corn shocks for our pumpkins. We put our pumpkins inside the shocks to keep them from freezing.

My brother and I always found fun things to do on the farm. We really liked those corn shocks because we could burrow back into them and make a nice cozy place to rest. The hayloft in the barn was another place in which we liked to play. It was fun jumping into the hay and making tunnels in it.

For a short time, we lived in Big Stone Gap, Virginia. It was there that I had my first experience with hot red pepper. In the loft of the barn, I saw several strings of long red pods of red peppers hanging to dry. I thought that one of them would make a nice balloon. I took one and tried to blow it up. You can imagine the rest of the story. I thought I was going to burn up.

Our home in Virginia was way out in the country, and we did not have an icebox, as it was called in those days. We kept our milk in half-gallon Mason canning jars and placed them in the stream that ran in front of the house to keep them cool. We took our corn to the old gristmill, which was powered by a large waterwheel. To get to the gristmill, we had to cross a long swinging bridge. As payment for grinding the corn, the miller took a certain amount of the cornmeal, which he then sold to the stores.

When I was small, freckles covered my face and I had red hair. At times, I was called "carrot top." In the backyard of one of our homes was a red cherry tree. One summer while I was up in the tree picking cherries, I slipped and fell. My stepmother told me that I came running into the house crying and said, "Your little red-headed boy just fell out of the cherry tree and killed himself." That obviously wasn't true because I am still here!

My stepmother was three-fourths Cherokee Indian. She really had many superstitious ideas. When my brother and I would stand behind an empty rocking chair and rock it, she would make us stop because she claimed that we were rocking someone out of the family. To her, it was bad luck to walk under a ladder propped up against a building. She also believed that a black cat crossing in front of you would bring bad luck unless you took ten steps backward before proceeding.

One of my stepmother's other superstitious ideas was that when you left home to go someplace, you should never return to get something that you had forgotten. If you did, you would have bad luck. One day, when we started out to go fishing at Fern Lake, she realized that we had forgotten something that we needed. We stopped on the hill to consider what to do. After a long time, she decided to return and get the bait we needed.

"I know that it is bad luck to turn back," she explained, "but if I don't, there is no need of our going fishing."

On our way to the lake, a terrible rainstorm came up. As we were standing on the roadside, a drunkard came along in his car and hit one of the poles holding the high-tension electrical wires. When he hit the pole, fire flew all around us. Mom swore it happened because we had turned back. How happy I am to know that in Psalm 17:5 that my heavenly Father has promised to "hold up my going in thy paths, that

Just a Kentucky Boy

my footsteps slip not."

After living in Virginia for a short time, we returned to Middlesboro because Dad was hired to be the janitor of the Middlesboro High School. He accepted the position only because my brother and I were given permission to attend the city school and help him with the janitorial work. Dad would leave for school about three o'clock in the morning. My brother and I would leave around five o'clock. Because there were no school buses at that time, we had to walk about three miles to school.

At home my brother and I took turns getting up early to build the fire so that Mom could get breakfast for Dad and us. Before we left, we had to make sure that the chickens were fed and that there was enough coal in the house to last until we got home in the evening.

After school we helped Dad clean the classrooms. The high school was three stories high with plenty of classrooms to clean. We usually returned home by 6:30 or 7:00 p.m. each evening. During Christmas break we had to wash all the windows in the school and handle any maintenance work that needed to be done. In the spring and summer, we had what seemed like acres of lawns and hedges to trim. During the summer Dad was responsible for taking care of the maintenance work in the entire city school system. Dad did not have much money, but he was determined that my brother and I would have a good education.

Part of what he considered as a good education was taking music lessons, so he rented two trombones for us to use so that we could be in the school band. I remember him saying, "Boys, I want you to learn how to play an instrument so that when you go into the armed service you will be able to carry a horn and not a gun."

We completed the elementary grades and entered high school. However, I had no interest in school. After one year and six weeks of high school, I persuaded my dad to petition the superintendent of schools to release me from school.

Chapter 2

Starting Out on My Own

At age 16 I left home to find my own place. I did not tell my brother, John my plans, which included drinking a big cup of black coffee to make myself sick so that I could miss school. After my brother left, I went to the fridge, got a big glass of cold buttermilk, and drank it to neutralize the acid from the coffee. I then left home and went to Morley, Tennessee, where I planned to stay with my stepmother's sister.

Brother John in Italy

My aunt lived about sixty miles from Oak Ridge, Tennessee, where I went to apply for a job. I found work as an exterminator with the Roan Anderson Company—killing rats, cockroaches, etc.—at fifty-eight cents an hour. After getting the job, I moved from my aunt's house to her stepdaughter's home in order to be closer to the road where I could get a ride to work each day. I left for work between 3:30 and 4:00 a.m. each day and arrive home between 7:00 and 8:00 each evening. Transportation on the military bus cost six dollars a week. Riding that old bus was really a challenge, especially in the winter. We often had to get out of the bus and push it up the icy road in order to get to work. As I received my paycheck each week, I would send part of it to my parents to help support them.

My first boss was a gentleman who had worked with the U.S. Public Health Department. As we would be driving along the road, he would stop the van and announce, "There's a rat burrow." After inspecting it, he could tell us the approximate number of rats living in that burrow.

In the summer we used HCN gas to exterminate rats. In the winter we used a large rubber hose, which we attached to the exhaust pipe of the van to flush out the rats. Inside buildings and under the large boardwalks, we used Red Squill rat poisoning mixed with sardines or ground beef. This was deadly to rats and mice, but it did not harm other small animals. It would kill the rats and mice because they were unable vomit.

We had another method we would use to exterminate rats. We would prop up the boardwalks, while my buddy would go to the farthes end of the walk and chase the rats up to where I waited. Lying down with a broomstick in hand, I would kill the rats as they came up through the opening of the boardwalk. You can kill a rat or mouse by hitting the sensitive blood vessel at the tip of their nose, causing them to bleed to death.

When World War II ended, Oak Ridge had grown into one of the largest cities in eastern Tennessee. The city played a large part in the development of the atomic bomb. As we worked around the various plants in Oak Ridge, we were not permitted to talk about anything that we observed. We were also warned of the possibility of sudden destruction occurring without notice. How thankful that my heavenly Father protected me in my Oak Ridge experience. His Word tells me in Psalm 46:1-3 that He is my refuge and strength.

Chapter 3

Military Life and the Army Band

When I turned 17, I asked my father to sign papers so that I could join the U.S. Army. Before leaving home, I made a commitment that, by God's grace, I would stop drinking and smoking. Dad used to make home brew in the basement of our house, and, of course, my brother and I sampled it. The first time I recall getting drunk was when we were visiting at the home of a neighbor. They had blackberry wine, and my brother and I, along with their children, got drunk on that blackberry wine. Also, my stepmother's brother sometimes visited us on the weekend, and I would go to town with him. Invariably, he would buy drinks and give some to me. One time I went with my stepbrother, Clem, and helped him carry moonshine from the mountain.

Only one time after I left home did I get drunk. It happened while sitting on the railroad trestle about a hundred feet from the tunnel in which a cousin and an uncle had been killed while drinking. It was while I sat there that the thought occurred to me that I could be next. I had been reading my Bible and knew that I should obey God. This experience made me realize that God was telling me that drinking was wrong. God gave me the strength to turn from those evil habits.

I passed my physical and was sworn into the U.S. Army at 4:55 p.m. on November 17, 1945, at Fort Oglethorpe, Georgia. I was sent to Fort McPherson in Atlanta for processing. I waited and waited to be called up, but my name was not mentioned. When I asked about it, they would say, "Just wait, soldier, your time will come."

After two weeks, when all those who were sworn in with me had been processed out, I asked, "When will I be processed out?"

They responded by asking, "Aren't you George Johnson?"

Each time this happened, I would tell them, "No, I am Harold Johnson."

Finally the sergeant said, "Come with me to headquarters."

When we reached headquarters, I was again asked my name, and again I assured them that I was Harold Johnson.

The officer said, "Are you sure that you are not George Johnson?"

Again, I assured them I was not. So they went and found George Johnson's packet, and lo and behold, my papers were inside. Someone had copied the name of the man before me onto my folder.

The officer looked at me with a grin and said, "Soldier, you have been AWOL for two weeks due to a typographical error!" Needless to say, they lost no time in processing me out. I was sent to Kessler Field in Biloxi, Mississippi, for basic training with the Army Air Corps. After basic training, I was sent to Chanute Field, Illinois, to weather school—in which I had no interest at all. After washing out of weather school, I was sent to the Pacific Theater of Operations as World War II was

Harold Johnson
13th Army Air Force

Military Life and the Army Band

coming to a close. There, my primary duty was guarding Japanese POWs who were younger than I. Soon after that my father's wish when I was in elementary school was fulfilled. The trombone lessons I had taken paid off. I was assigned to the 600th Army Air Corps Band at Clark Field in the Philippines. I played trombone in the regular band and the dance band, where I received a dollar an hour and free drinks.

When I entered the Army, my buddies tried to get me to drink, but I refused each time. They said, "After you have been in the Army for six weeks, you will be like the rest of us, smoking and drinking."

However, I remembered my commitment to my stepmother and to God, and I never drank anything but soft drinks. One time when I was playing a dance program at the Enlisted Men's Club at Clark Field, we were told that they could not serve us alcoholic drinks because of some problem the night before. When break time came, they brought out soft drinks and asked each of us what we would like. I chose a Coke. But after they popped the top off and I took one swallow, I knew that I had more than a Coke! They had spiked all the drinks. I immediately requested a plain Coke.

Years later, after I became a Seventh-day Adventist, the fellows in my outfit kept teasing me about drinking a beer. They kept after me, asking me to have a beer with them. Finally, I consented to have just one beer with them on my birthday, but I did not tell them when my birthday was. They found out anyway, and on my birthday, they reminded me of my promise to have one beer with them.

"OK," I told them. "I will not lie to you. I will keep my promise and drink one beer."

So we went to the Post Exchange for a beer. They ordered theirs: Miller, Pabst Blue Ribbon, Budweiser, etc. When the waiter asked me what I wanted to drink, I said, "I would like a root beer, please." The fellows immediately jumped on me verbally, but I told them that all I

Just a Kentucky Boy

had agreed to do was drink a beer—I had never specified what kind. That ended the teasing in the service and afterward.

Because of my integrity and hard work, I won the confidence of my commanding officer and fellow servicemen. One time my commander gave me the payroll, which had not all been dispersed on payday, which was a Friday. He asked me to keep it until Monday when the rest of the men would be back from their leaves. According to Army regulations, the payroll that remained was to be returned to the Post Finance, but it was late and the office was closed. I was really concerned about being responsible for that large amount of money; yet, all went well until I could return it to my commander on Monday morning.

Late one night when the fellows returned from a drinking spree in town, one of them came to my barracks and awakened me. I asked him what he wanted. "I want you to come over to my barracks with me," he said. I dressed and went to his barrack, and he said, "I want you to pray for me."

I knelt by his bed and prayed for him. When I finished, he stood up, looked me straight in the eye, and said, "I didn't think you would do it!" Then, handing me a whiskey bottle with about a third left, he said, "This is the end." Whether or not he kept his promise, I am not sure. I did not remain much longer at that camp because the time drew near for my discharge from the service.

But before my discharge, I was able to accomplish two promises I had made to my dad before shipping out to the Philippines. I had made a commitment to have stripes on my arm and my high school diploma before coming home. As I mentioned, in the Philippines, I was assigned to the 600th Army Air Corps Band as a trombone player. However, the tuba player was soon to return to the States, so the bandleader promised me that if I would learn to play the tuba before

Military Life and the Army Band

the tuba player left he would make it worth my while. Needless to say, I began learning how to play the tuba, and by the time the tuba player left for the States, I was ready to take his position. I often bragged that I was the best tuba player in the band and also the worst because I was the only one! The bandleader kept his word, and I was awarded two stripes instead of one, making me a corporal.

After that I fulfilled the second part of my promise to Dad by completing my high school education through the United States Armed Forces Institute. I graduated in May 1947, the year I should have graduated from Middlesboro High School if I had stayed in school. But since dropping out, I had completed two years of mandatory service in the Army, and one year of work experience. Furthermore, I had three stripes on my arm when I returned home. I had more than honored my commitment to Dad.

After being discharged from the service, I got a job working with A. B. Pest Control, a local company in my hometown. After several weeks of work, my boss invited me to his church for a revival meeting. I accepted the invitation.

When he asked me where I would like to sit, I said, "Up close to the front of the church."

We walked up to the first pew and sat down. When the pastor finished his preaching, he gave a call to prayer. Because it was a Pentecostal church, everyone began praying out loud. My boss and I joined in the prayer service. My boss finished before I did, and he began talking to the gentleman next to him, telling him about all the new jobs we had secured in the past few days and how much money the company would be getting. Although I was not very religious, his behavior did not sit well with me. It seemed quite inappropriate when many of the members were "getting the Holy Spirit." After that experience, I decided not to go to church with him again.

Just a Kentucky Boy

Although I didn't go back to church with him, I was interested in spiritual matters, and I began listening to *The Voice of Prophecy* radio program, which I first heard in the Philippines. A little while later after my boss found out what I was listening to, he told me that he and his wife were really worried about me getting mixed up in the cults. I assured him that if *The Voice of Prophecy* was a cult I was rather interested in it because they were really preaching from the Word. After that discussion, our relationship began to grow cold.

Finally, I quit working with him and got a job ushering in the theater. I went to work at ten in the morning and got off after the last movie, about half past eleven at night. For that, I was paid thirteen dollars a week.

One day I said to my father, "You know, this is foolish to be working these long hours for such low pay. I can do better than this in the Army and work fewer hours."

So I joined the Army again. As I was preparing to board the bus for Fort Knox, Kentucky, my father said, "Son, I believe that you should send your tithe and offerings to *The Voice of Prophecy*, for they are doing more good than anyone else."

After completing a three-week refresher course at Fort Knox, I was assigned to the 3rd Armored Division Band and Band Training School. I played tuba in the main band and received my certificate of completion from the Band Training Unit. I also served as the Supply Sergeant for the band and for the training school.

After completing my refresher course and being assigned to the 3rd Armored Division Band, I recalled my father's advice and began sending money to *The Voice of Prophecy*. One day I finally got up the nerve to ask for one of the Bible courses. I felt that my best bet was to take the junior course. After completing that, I requested the senior course. I completed that, too, and asked for the advanced course

Military Life and the Army Band

on Daniel and Revelation. I had heard that there was a Seventh-day Adventist Church in Elizabethtown, Kentucky, just about twenty miles from Fort Knox, but I could not find anyone who knew anything about it.

Finally, I located information about the church and the pastor, Ralph Ricks, came to the barracks to visit me. After discussing many things, he invited me to church the next Sabbath. Attending was not a problem because we seldom had to work on Sabbath. I began attending church in "E-town," as it was called. The church had not yet been organized at that time, and when it was, I became a charter member, as well as one of the deacons. I was baptized on January 1, 1949, in the Louisville, Kentucky, church by Pastor Calvin Osborn. Pastor Ricks could not baptize me because he had not yet been ordained. I was his first convert to the Seventh-day Adventist Church. It wasn't until I joined the church that I learned that my dad had grown up as a Seventh-day Adventist and had been a charter member of the church in Rockford, Indiana.

My baptism was the culmination of a spiritual journey that actually began in the Philippines. While stationed overseas, each week I listened to three religious programs on my radio—*The Old-fashioned Revival Hour, The Lutheran Hour*, and *The Voice of Prophecy*. In addition to the radio programs, I had a few *Voice of Prophecy* books. I purchased them from a young Filipino girl who was standing in front of a store in Manila. I was simply walking the streets when she approached me and asked if I would like to buy a book. I asked her what kind of book, and she showed them to me. When I asked her how much, she said, "Fifty centavos." They looked like the *Voice of Prophecy* books I had seen in my aunt's house, so I bought three from her. I count that as my first experience in becoming a Seventh-day Adventist. Each week, I always looked forward to hearing Pastor Richard's sermon and the

Just a Kentucky Boy

King's Heralds' songs on the radio.

Although I did not have to work on Sabbath, there was one event that caused some problems once I became a Seventh-day Adventist. The 3rd Armored Division Band represented the United States at the Kentucky Derby by playing the National Anthem just before the race began. We always had the privilege of having ringside seats for the races all day long—I had the privilege of being there when Citation won the race. Of course, the Kentucky Derby is always run on the first Saturday in May, which was fine until I joined the church. Once I became a Seventh-day Adventist, I knew that I must keep the Sabbath instead of play for the races. My commanding officer was sympathetic, but not my first sergeant, who set in motion a plan to have me shipped out.

Now I had a problem to solve! First, I checked with the post bandleader who said that he would be happy to have me in his band, but unfortunately, he had no opening for a tuba player at that time. He suggested that I contact Chief Warrant Officer Jeffries at Aberdeen Proving Ground in Maryland. I knew Mr. Jeffries very well since I had been his supply sergeant when he was head of the Band Training Unit at Fort Knox. I asked permission of my first sergeant and commander to contact Mr. Jeffries, but the request was denied. Next, I asked the post chaplain for advice. He suggested that I contact the inspector general of Fort Knox. When I contacted him, he asked what I would like to do. I told him that I would like permission to contact Mr. Jeffries at Aberdeen Proving Ground to see if he would accept me. The inspector general put a hold on all orders for me until I heard from Mr. Jeffries. Because this irritated my first sergeant, I waited approximately two years before they let me know that Mr. Jeffries had accepted me.

Upon my arrival at Aberdeen Proving Ground, I was assigned to the 324th Army Band. Mr. Jeffries could not understand why it took

Military Life and the Army Band

so long for me to get there, for he had replied almost immediately. Besides being a band member, I was assigned as assistant supply sergeant and as unit mail clerk. There were no real Sabbath problems. However, because I was never there for inspection on Sabbath, I was assigned to permanent latrine duty, which did not bother me because I had always passed the inspections without any trouble. Our band was scheduled for every Saturday evening to play a thirty-minute concert at a TV station in Baltimore. That never presented a problem because the Sabbath was always over before the beginning of the program.

Then, it finally happened—a Sabbath issue arose! President Truman was coming for a visit to Aberdeen Proving Ground on Sabbath, and I was given direct orders from my commanding officer that I would have to be there for the honors.

When I told Mr. Jeffries that I could not be there, he said, "Well, this is the only time you will have to do it. It will probably never happen again."

"You may be right, sir," I replied, "but it could happen again next Sabbath."

"Well, I am giving you a direct order," he repeated. "You will play tomorrow."

I fully recognized what this "direct order" could mean to my military career. However, I determined that I would follow the direct order that is given in Exodus 20: 8-11 to "Remember the Sabbath day to keep it holy." I thanked him and left.

At that time I was a member of the Blythedale Seventh-day Adventist Church. On Friday evening I went to the young adult meeting and talked with Pastor Cunningham about my dilemma. He suggested that we go see the head chaplain, but we could not find him. Then Pastor Cunningham suggested that we go visit my commanding officer. We found where he lived and talked with him, but he would not yield.

"What will you do if he does not play?" Pastor Cunningham asked.

I knew what his answer would be from having worked with him at Fort Knox. Mr. Jeffries replied, "He will be of no use to me. I will ship him out."

While we were talking, Mr. Jeffries' wife came down from upstairs and went in the dining room with their small son. Seeing that we were not making any progress, we thanked him for his time and left. Just as we were leaving, he remarked, "If I change my mind, I will let you know in the morning."

Pastor Cunningham called the conference officers and had them pray for me, and all the area churches were praying for me. That night as my colleagues came in from their trip into town, I heard them asking each other, "What will Johnson do? We can't get off on Sunday; we have always worked on Sundays when needed, but he has never worked on Saturday."

The next morning it was raining quite hard, and the church members were sure that the Lord had answered their prayers. What they did not realize was that rain does not stop the armed forces. While the men were getting dressed for the parade, I lay on my bunk and prayed. At around nine o'clock, I was called to report to the commanding officer.

When I arrived, his first words were, "Do you remember what we talked about last night?"

"Yes, sir," I responded. How could I forget?

"Well, after you left last night," he continued, "my wife and I talked together, and she told me that she had some very close friends who were Seventh-day Adventists, and she said that they are very strict in their beliefs. So we decided to let you off this time."

You can imagine how I felt when I left for church that morning! I always had to hitchhike to church, but that morning I did not have

Military Life and the Army Band

to wait long for a ride. You should have seen the looks on the faces of the church members when I walked in! The rain had stopped, and the sun was shining brightly. Truly, it was a modern-day Pilate's wife who came to the rescue, all because of a faithful Seventh-day Adventist friend.

On Monday morning when I went to pick up the mail, my commander called me into his office and asked me to pick up some stamps for him. "Do you remember what we talked about Saturday morning?" he asked. "Well, when a good opportunity comes around, we will see what we can work out for you." Not only had I received my Sabbath off, but I was being honored for my faithfulness and loyalty to my faith and my position in the Army. Shortly after that, I received orders from headquarters presenting me with the Good Conduct Medal.

After this experience, I went to the post chaplain and told him that I was a Seventh-day Adventist and would appreciate any help he could give me to make it possible for me to keep the Sabbath.

"Soldier," he said, "I can't do anything for you until I get a notarized letter from your pastor stating that you are a Seventh-day Adventist in good standing at your church."

I thanked him and immediately went to Pastor Cunningham, got the letter, had it notarized, and took it back to the chaplain.

When he saw me, he remarked, "You really meant business, didn't you?"

Several weeks later, my commander called me into his office and informed me of an Army regulation that stated that the commander could request for me to be reclassified as a conscientious objector, noncombatant, if I wanted him to send a letter to that effect. I agreed with his suggestion, so he issued the letter and I was reclassified as a conscientious objector. When it came time for my discharge, my commander and first sergeant pled with me to re-enlist and stay with them.

"We need men like you," they said.

Nevertheless, I did not re-enlist, and I was discharged on March 1, 1951.

Chapter 4

School, School, and More School

With my discharge from the Army, I decided to take a different route with my life and pursue an education. My plan was to enroll at Madison College in Nashville, Tennessee. On my way I stopped at Highlands Academy to visit my nephew—I was hoping he would become a Seventh-day Adventist. While I talked with Pastor Strickland, the principal, he asked me what my plans were. When I told him that I was thinking of going to Madison College, he assured me that what I really needed to do was attend Southern Missionary College in Collegedale, Tennessee.

"I have a friend there who will help you," he said.

Thus convinced, the next morning I changed plans and headed to Southern Missionary College. When I arrived in Chattanooga, Tennessee, R. C. Mizelle met me at the bus station and took me to Collegedale. He introduced me to Dr. Rittenhouse, the academic dean. When I told Dr. Rittenhouse I was hoping to enroll in school in order to keep from losing my WWII GI bill benefits, he said, "I don't see any reason why you cannot enroll now."

It was right at the time when the midterm tests for the second semester were being administered, but I enrolled for nine semester hours of work. That meant that I would need to catch up on the first half of the semester's work for those nine hours. This was rather a challenge for one who had once said, "I will never go back to school again."

Studying was not my only challenge. Financing my college education was also difficult. I had to borrow fifty dollars for the entrance fee because I had no money. I was assigned work in the broom shop. I worked every chance I had. Before my discharge, I had been told that in order to keep my GI bill benefits I would need to be enrolled in a school. I received permission to enroll with the Home Study Institute with the assurance that, upon my discharge, I could transfer to a school of my choice. I took twelve hours of college work from Home Study Institute; however, when I got to Southern Missionary College, my request to transfer to the college was refused. For the convenience of the government, my term of service had been extended for an extra year because of the Korean Conflict, which put me over the deadline for receiving the World War II GI bill.

In spite of these difficulties, when the semester was over, I had successfully completed nine semester hours of college work. Still hoping that my request would be granted, I decided to take summer school. Since I had an outstanding bill, the business office did not want to grant me permission to take summer school. I explained to them that I was sure that the GI bill would come through for me. With that assurance, I was granted permission to enroll. When summer school was over, I had successfully worked off my bill and had fifty dollars for the entrance fee for the first semester of the new school year, so I enrolled, still hoping that the GI bill benefits would come through. Unfortunately, it never happened. Fearing, from the beginning, that the GI bill benefits would never materialize, I had changed my course from theology to elementary education.

Therefore, when the second semester arrived, I figured that I would be unable to register. However, during the weeks before the

School, School, and More School

beginning of the second semester, I had made friends with a young lady by the name of Marjorie Connell. Knowing about my dilemma, she told her parents about my situation. Unbeknown to me, they came to my rescue. I was allowed to register for the second semester because of her parents' financial assistance. In addition, I worked in the broom shop, in the dorm, and at any odd jobs I could find to make sure my school bills were paid—I also was sending money home each month to help support my parents.

Marjorie and I became friends because some of our classmates urged us to get to know each other. As the second semester began, our friends concocted a scheme to help us get "better acquainted." It was a leap year, and to celebrate it, the school planned a special program that enabled the young ladies to invite a friend—the custom was known as "reverse dating." Unbeknownst to Marjorie, one of her friends sent me a note as if it were from her asking me for a date. My acceptance of it was the beginning of our becoming "better acquainted."

Sometime after that, the girls asked me if I would like to go snipe hunting with them and Marjorie. I played dumb (I knew that snipe hunting was a type of practical joke), so I asked them what snipe hunting was all about. They explained it to us, and Marjorie and I agreed to go.

When we got to the woods behind the dormitory, they told us that we were to hold the bag. They left us there while they went on to find the snipes and chase them in toward us. Then I explained to Marjorie what it was all about—that there would be no snipes and we would be left "holding the bag." Chuckling, we headed for the dormitory another way. You can imagine the surprise of the other girls when they returned for us and we were not there!

Marjorie and I quickly became special friends, especially when I mentioned that I knew Archie Rawson Jr., who turned out to be her cousin. Our friendship grew over the next few months. While I was visiting her and her parents in Wytheville, Virginia, we took a walk into the cow pasture by her home. In the course of our conversation, I asked her what she planned to do after graduating in the spring. She said that she would probably find a teaching job somewhere. Since I, too, would be graduating with my diploma in elementary education, I asked her what she thought about our teaching together. She seemed to think that was a good idea. Upon our return from the walk, I asked her parents for permission to marry their daughter. They readily agreed and the engagement was sealed.

The rest of the semester flew by, especially since we would spend our Sabbaths helping out in seminar meetings held in small churches in the area. Marjorie would provide the special music, and I would lead out in the service.

Marjorie graduated in the spring, and I graduated with the summer class of 1953, having completed all requirements for a two-year diploma in elementary education. This was a milestone I had never expected to reach. After graduation I walked into the registrar's office and picked up my diploma. The next morning I walked into the business office and picked up $250, my earnings over and above my college expenses. It is marvelous what our heavenly Father can do—even for a Kentucky boy. Especially when we claim the promise of 1 Peter 5:7 "Casting all your care upon Him; for He careth for you."

Before graduation, we applied for jobs and received calls to teach in Arkansas, Indiana, Virginia, South Carolina, New Mexico, and Florida. Our final choice was Panama City, Florida.

After my summer graduation, Marjorie Ethel Connell became my beloved wife on August 17, 1953, in Wytheville, Virginia. Pastor Oliver Jacques performed the service. After a short honeymoon at Hungry Mother's State Park in Virginia, we loaded our few belongings into a

School, School, and More School

small trailer. Mother and Daddy Connell drove with us to Panama City where we began our teaching career together.

Unfortunately, the school in Panama City was not able to support two teachers, so after one year we took a job teaching in Greenville, Tennessee. Because I only had a two-year diploma in education, the conference sent me to summer school each year to work toward my degree. While going to summer school, I was given the privilege of working as assistant dean of men for the academy and college students at Southern Missionary College. At that time, they all lived together in Talge Hall. This was my privilege for five summers. After teaching for three years in Greenville, we moved to Pewee Valley, Kentucky, and taught there for one year.

After that I decided to take one year off to complete my degree. Again, the Lord blessed me by giving me the opportunity of being assistant to the dean of men for the college, as well as dean of boys for the academy, which had been moved to an old building in back of Talge Hall and renamed Amekie Hall. The boys lived on the top floor, and the classrooms were on the first floor. That was a very busy year for me, as well as for Marjorie. Not only was she to be nurse to the boys but she also assisted with teaching the home economics classes. I was busy working on a double major, education and religion, and a minor in secondary education. Because of the religion major, I spent many Sabbath mornings helping conduct services in the surrounding churches.

Keeping up with school took a lot of dedication, but graduation was right around the corner.

Chapter 5

From Georgia to the Middle East

After graduation, the Georgia-Cumberland Conference asked me to teach in Marietta, Georgia. During that summer, I also served as the pastor of the church in Rome, Georgia. When the school year began, I taught in Marietta and also worked as assistant to Pastor E. A. Crain, who cared for the churches in Marietta, Rome, and Cedartown. After teaching in Marietta for one year, I was invited to be the principal for the Adventist school in Chattanooga, Tennessee.

We moved once again and established ourselves in Chattanooga, but unknown to us, we were about to embark on another journey. While teaching in Chattanooga, we were approached by the General Conference Mission Board to consider a call to the Sudan in Africa. There had never been a Seventh-day Adventist missionary in the Sudan, we were told, and sending us there was only a hopeful venture. We accepted the challenge, received the call from the General Conference, and ventured to Africa to open up temperance and welfare work in the Sudan.

Traveling to a mission field can prove to be an adventure in itself. When we finally sailed from New York, after having five sailing dates, we were prepared to be aboard the ship for about three weeks. Our first stop was in Alexandria, Egypt. From there, we continued to Beirut, Lebanon, where we were able to get off the ship for a short time.

From Georgia to the Middle East

Pastor Kenneth Oster met us and took us to the Middle East Division Office for a visit. Since we still had a little time before we had to board the ship again, the Osters took us to pay a quick visit to the ruins of Baalbek. Next, we sailed for the Suez Canal. There our ship was delayed for twenty-four hours because two ships had collided and blocked the passageway.

The ship was scheduled to stop at Aquaba, Jordan, to unload some freight. But by the time the ship arrived at the mouth of the Gulf of Aquaba, it was dark. The captain of the ship did not want to wait until daylight to travel up the gulf because there was danger of being robbed. Entering the gulf was dangerous because ships had been sunk at the entrance to prevent warships from entering. The captain had the spotlights turned on, and he slowly steered the ship through the treacherous entrance. The ship arrived safely at the port the next morning to unload the freight.

After leaving Aquaba, we sailed for Port Sudan. We thought that we would soon reach our destination, but when we arrived, there was no room for the ship to dock. Passengers were taken ashore in small rowboats. The Nile Union president was supposed to have been there to meet us, but a severe rainstorm had washed out the airstrip, and the plane could not land. What a disappointment! We had to go through customs without the help of someone who knew the ropes.

Customs was somewhat of a nightmare! First, we were asked to declare our goods. After we had declared what we had, the customs officials figured out how much the customs charge would be, it came to about three thousand pounds sterling, approximately $6,900 in U.S. dollars.

"That is too much!" the Sudanese official exclaimed. "Can you wait for an hour? We will figure it out again."

"Yes," we assured him, "we can wait."

Just a Kentucky Boy

After an hour the same officer returned, and we made our declaration again. He asked about wedding gifts, household articles, clothing, and other articles for which there would be no charge because they were used items.

"Do you have any food?" he asked.

"We did bring along several cases of food," I admitted.

"Used!" he said, with a pencil poised over his paper.

"We haven't even tasted it yet!" I protested.

He laughed and said, "I guess it will have to be new."

There were several other things we had that really were new, but when we told the customs authority about an item being new, he would say, "I said used." And that was what was written by those items! The biggest charges were for the projector and for equipment that we were taking in for the mission. After all was figured up, the total customs charges this time were only three hundred pounds sterling, or $690 in U.S. dollars.

Reservations were supposed to have been made for us in the Port Sudan Hotel, but someone had failed to make them. When we tried to register, there were no rooms available. Fortunately, while we waited, wondering what to do, the train left for Khartoum. Some of the hotel guests departed on that train, leaving some vacancies. That solved our immediate problem.

After three days, Pastor Gordon Zytkoskee, the Nile Union president, was finally able to fly into Port Sudan to meet us. On Sabbath afternoon we took a walk along the Indian Ocean. We did not realize how far we had walked until we noticed the time. Because it was too far for us to walk back in time for the evening meal, we looked around for another option of transportation. We saw a Sudanese with his small boat, and we thought he could take us back to the hotel. But we could not speak Arabic, and we could not get him to understand what we wanted. There was another man a short distance away having evening prayer who stopped praying and came over to translate for us. We agreed to pay for the trip after the Sabbath, so we got our ride and our meal. When the sun had set, we went down to the waterfront and paid the gentlemen for his services. The next day we flew Sudan Airways to Khartoum where we stayed in a hotel until we could find a place to live.

It was Christmas and our shipment had not yet arrived. Marjorie and I thought that we would splurge. For our Christmas dinner, we bought half a dozen eggs, which we boiled on a small kerosene stove loaned to us by our landlord. When we were ready to eat them, we sadly discovered that they were spoiled. Therefore, for our Christmas treat, we went to the hotel, had a glass of lemonade each, and bought a *Reader's Digest* for Marjorie. We had many a laugh remembering our Christmas dinner in December 1961.

We had to live for some time without our household goods. When they finally did arrive, we were missing our kitchen stove. It had been sent to Asmara, Ethiopia. When it finally arrived, the only address on it was "Harold Johnson, Sudan, Africa."

As it turned out, we were not there long enough to accomplish anything except for a few weeks of language study. The government of Sudan had given us temporary permits for only three months.

Unfortunately, before the three months were up, the government refused to renew our permits. Due to a conflict between the two major religious groups in the country, the government expelled all foreign missionaries from the country. We were given fifteen days to leave, but by the time I received the registered letter from the post office with the notice, there were only thirteen days left.

Thirteen days were not enough time! I petitioned the government to give us an extension to the expulsion date, but I never heard from them. The division wanted us to travel by ship or train to Egypt, but that was impossible. All reservations were booked for months in advance. It was about a month before we could get a flight out of the country to Cairo, Egypt. Meanwhile, we had to get export licenses for all of the things we owned. I had failed to list a Zenith radio that my brother had given us—a radio he had had while serving in Korea—so we had to leave it behind. The day arrived for us to leave, but our household belongings could not be shipped for over a month, so we had to walk out of the house and leave all our earthly belongings except what we could carry.

Pastor Zytkoskee and Pastor Raymond Hartwell, the division secretary, met us when we arrived in Cairo. The plan was for us to go to Jordan because, at that time, the Jordanian government was granting gratis visas to Americans. Upon our arrival, the president of the Jordanian Mission asked me to serve as acting secretary-treasurer. What a challenge for an elementary school teacher! I survived the ordeal, with much help, for about six weeks. Next, the division asked me to go to the Middle East College in Beirut, Lebanon, to teach in the religion and education department. I readily accepted—that was a job I was familiar with! I readily accepted the words of 2 Timothy 2:15 "Study to show thyself approved unto God, a workman that needeth not to be ashamed, rightly dividing the Word of truth."

Although I was sent to Beirut as a college teacher, the next few years proved to be full of unexpected changes. As soon as we arrived, Pastor G. Arthur Keough, the division educational secretary, requested that the college grant me a leave of absence to teach the Beirut Overseas School for a year to replace Izella Stuivenga while she was on furlough. That year, I taught grades five through eight. When the school year ended, I was asked to teach summer school classes at the college. After summer school Pastor Keough decided that I would not teach in the college but remain as principal of the Beirut Overseas School. Another change occurred in my job assignment when Pastor Keough was appointed as president of Middle East College. Shortly after assuming the presidency, he changed his mind and decided that I would be a teacher at the college. During the preceding year, the pastor of the Middle East College Church, Pastor Kenneth Oster, had resigned to accept a call to Iran. The Lebanese Mission appointed me as pastor of the church, the largest church in the division at that time. That responsibility, added to my teaching, really kept me busy.

The next year life became even more complicated. The registrar and her husband left for the United States to get their master's degrees. I was asked to be registrar for the college and the secondary school in addition to serving as pastor of the church and teaching Bible and education classes. If that weren't enough, since there were a few extra hours left in the day and there was a need for an upper grade teacher in the Beirut Overseas School, I was asked to teach grades five through seven in the mornings.

That year my day went something like this: I would teach in the Beirut Overseas School beginning at eight o'clock in the morning. At noon a division worker would pick me up and take me to my home at the college where Marjorie would have lunch ready. I would eat and head down to the college for my one o'clock afternoon class. It was quite a challenge to shift gears from teaching elementary classes to teaching college classes. After an afternoon of teachings, I then had to handle my registrar and pastoral duties.

Perhaps the most important events during this time were the births of our two children. In keeping with Arabic tradition, Stephen was born first. I put a note about his birth on the college bulletin board. Later, when Karen joined the family, life seemed complete. In celebration, I put a box of chocolates on my desk in the registrar's office and invited those who came in to have a chocolate. When anyone asked what the chocolates were for, I would tell them that my wife had given birth to a baby girl. Invariably, the next question was, "Why chocolates for the girl and nothing for the boy?"

The custom in the Middle East was to rejoice when a son was born but almost keep it a secret when a daughter was born. Each time the question was asked, I would explain that I have always had a soft spot in my heart for little girls because my mother was one. They could not argue with that.

An interesting fact is that Stephen almost shared a birthday with the present king of Jordan, King Abdullah. Stephen and Karen's doctor was an Armenian lady on the staff of the American University Hospital in Beirut. She was also the private doctor for the wife of King Hussein. Stephen was born in December, and the present king of Jordan, King Abdullah, was born a month later in January.

We had survived the first five-year term in the mission field and were making plans for our furlough. The college wanted me to go to Andrews University and get my master's degree. We had made plans to do just that when I received word that my mother was to have major surgery—she was to have one of her lungs removed. That meant that I would be responsible for helping with her medical bills. The General Conference committee suggested that the Middle East Division should help me with my financial crisis, but the division refused.

Since the Middle East Division was unable to help with my educational expenses or my mother's medical bills, my plans had to change. I was given the name of a Baptist school in Atlanta, Georgia, where I could get my master's degree much cheaper than at Andrews. And we would be close to Marjorie's folks. The president of the school, having an aunt who was a Seventh-day-Adventist, was willing to accept me as a student even though I was a member of the Seventh-

From Georgia to the Middle East

day Adventist Church and not a Baptist. I gave the General Conference all the information and was granted approval for pursuing my master's degree at the Baptist school.

The General Conference promised to notify the Middle East Division of the plan. When the division heard of this plan, they told us that I could not return as a faculty member if I obtained a degree from a school outside of the Seventh-day Adventist denomination. I went ahead, however, with my plans, and after spending a few years in school, I received a bachelor of divinity and a master's degree in religious education.

When the West Virginia Conference heard that I was without a job, they extended a call to me to pastor the three churches in the Richwood District—Richwood, Webster Springs, and East Ranell. While serving in that district, I made it a priority to speak in all three churches each Sabbath. My first service started at 9:00 a.m. at Webster Springs; my second service was at Richwood at 11:30 a.m.; and then we drove to East Ranell for Sabbath School and a final worship service beginning at 2:00 p.m. Our accomplishments while there included helping to build a new church in East Ranell and securing property in Richwood for a future church building.

We had been in West Virginia for about a year when we received a call from the General Conference requesting that we fill the position of principal at the Beirut Overseas School. With that call began another period of confusion. We had been told that we could not come back, but when we moved back to the States, we had to leave all our worldly possessions in storage in Beirut. So we accepted the call, knowing that our household items were waiting for us. In the meantime, the General Conference was in session, and unbeknown to the new secretary of education for the Middle East Division, they had called another person to be principal of the Beirut Overseas School, not realizing that we had

Just a Kentucky Boy

already accepted the call.

We discovered the problem on the ship while heading for the Middle East. We met two other families on board who were going to the same location. As we talked together, I asked them about their assignments. Dale Hepker was to be dean of men at Middle East College. Jim Stephan was to be principal of the Beirut Overseas School. When they asked me what I was to be doing, I answered, "I am to be a teacher at the Beirut Overseas School."

Although we were having a good school year, there was political unrest in the country. The conflict between the Arabs and the Israelis was growing stronger. As things heated up and the possibility of war loomed before us, the division requested that we have our suitcases packed and ready to go at a moment's notice. We did have our suitcases packed and ready to go, but we later discovered that we had forgotten our toothbrushes!

We were living off the compound when we were told to be ready for evacuation in the morning. Since we always liked listening to music, that night I decided to record some tapes to take with us. We had just a little bubble bath left, so we put the children in the bathtub to play. Shortly after that there was a knock at the door. Upon opening the door, we discovered that it was one of the division workers. "Let's go. I have come for you. You are being evacuated immediately."

Obviously, we had not expected to be evacuated until morning. Not living on the compound, we had not received notice of the change in plans. It took us about thirty minutes to snatch the children from the tub, dress them, and grab whatever music tapes were done along with our suitcases. What a strange feeling it was to walk out of our house and leave everything behind, not knowing whether or not we would ever see it again! We carried four things with us—two suitcases with our clothes, one suitcase with our Sabbath felts, and Marjorie's featherweight Singer sewing machine.

"I can always make clothes for the children regardless of where we are, and we can always use the Sabbath materials as well," Marjorie said.

Finally, it erupted in June of 1967—the Arab-Israeli Six-Day War, and we found ourselves in the middle of war which brought to my mind the words of Mark 13:7 "And when ye shall hear of wars and rumors of wars, be ye not troubled, for such things must needs be; but the end shall not be yet." All missionaries had been sent to the American University in Beirut as a gathering place in preparation for evacuation. Dr. Horn was with us. He had been on his way to a dig in Jordan, but now his plans were changed. As we gathered together there in the room, he exclaimed, "What a way for one to spend his anniversary!"

Around midnight there was a terrific explosion in the Beirut harbor. Someone had blown up a large fuel storage tank. Immediately, all heads of families were called down to a large assembly room. We were informed that immediate plans were being made to evacuate everyone by air. We were instructed to immediately get everything ready to leave for the airport. As we all turned to follow the directions, the parting injunction was, "For God's sake, don't forget the children." We were given tags with which to label Stephen and Karen so that their identity would be clear in case they got separated from us. We were loaded into buses for the trip to the airport. It was a total blackout. Soldiers were in the bus, behind it, in front of it, and along either side of it. All we were allowed to take with us was what we could carry. Having two small children, Marjorie and I could not carry much. We did not know where we were going or how long we would be gone. We wore our regular clothes, as well as our heavy winter coats.

Just a Kentucky Boy

At the airport at daybreak, we saw the first Pan American 707 touchdown, and shortly thereafter, the second, and then, the third. We boarded the second plane. Just as soon as it was loaded, it took off and lost no time in heading out over the international waters of the Mediterranean Sea. Later, we were told that we were flying to Istanbul, Turkey. When we landed at Istanbul, we were put on buses that took us up the Bosporus to a large, modern hotel.

In times of crisis, it is easy to lose track of time. After three days or so, a lady came up to me and asked, "Can you please tell me what day this is?"

Later, we were all taken into Istanbul to a hotel where we could be together with all the division missionaries. After many contacts with the General Conference in Washington, D.C., we were told that we all must take our vacations now since there would be none when we returned to our various fields of labor. Marjorie and I decided that we would like to take our vacation on the island of Cyprus. After a long, all-day flight on Turkish Air, we finally arrived in Cyprus. We stayed in a hotel in Nicosia. Three days after our arrival, all the division personnel who had been evacuated were moved to Cyprus because it was closer to the division headquarters in Beirut. While there, Pastor Jim Russell and I took the opportunity to retrace the footsteps of the apostle Paul and Barnabas on their missionary trip on the island.

Not knowing when we would ever get back into Beirut, the division asked Marjorie and me to go to Iran and teach in the Iranian Training School. We received permission to return to Beirut long enough to pack our things for shipment to Iran. Needless to say, the U.S. Embassy in Beirut was not pleased to know that we were there, and they were very happy when we left!

When we arrived in Iran, we discovered that the teacher for the missionary children had resigned. Again, our plans had to change!

From Georgia to the Middle East

Iran would not admit an ex-patriot just to teach, so I was assigned to be pastor of the Farsee Church in Teheran, as well as to be the teacher for the school. In the meantime, the director of the Tehran Evangelistic Center resigned. I was asked to be acting director. That meant that I had three half-time jobs to juggle! While in Iran I was ordained to the gospel ministry.

Oren G. Johnson
Father (Deceased)

It was also while we were in Iran that my dad passed away. I received the news after church one Sabbath when I arrived home. Our gardener handed me a telegram from my brother, John. Dad had passed away on Thursday, and the funeral was scheduled for that Sabbath at 1 p.m. in the States. He was buried in a cemetery in Middlesboro, Kentucky. It was not easy being across the ocean while my family was coping with my father's death back home, but I couldn't travel back to the States.

It took awhile, but things finally calmed down somewhat in Lebanon. After spending two years in Iran, we were asked to return to teach in the Beirut Overseas School again. We settled into a routine, but after one year there, Marjorie was diagnosed with breast cancer. After her surgery at the American University Hospital in Beirut, we were issued a permanent medical return to the United States. Our life was about to change again.

Chapter 6

New Beginnings

We arrived back on American soil, and my first assignment was teaching in Fort Pierce, Florida. After a year there, we were transferred to Tri-City Junior Academy in North Carolina. During that year Marjorie's cancer worsened, making it necessary for us to leave North Carolina in order to get the medical treatments she needed. We went to Wildwood Lifestyle Center and Hospital in Georgia so that Marjorie could receive the medical care she needed. This also brought us closer to her parents.

Because of our uncertain situation, none of the conferences were willing to hire me; consequently, the General Conference assigned me to Laurelbrook School, a self-supporting school in Dayton, Tennessee. Once again, I was given a variety of responsibilities. I was hired to serve as chaplain for the school and sanitarium, as pastor of the church, as Bible teacher for the academy, and as principal for the elementary school.

Laurelbrook School housed the Laymen's Foundation Educational Institution, it served as an extension school for the laymen's foundation with Southern Missionary College. In addition to my many duties, I served as vice president for the Laurelbrook School and liaison officer between the college and the Laymen's Foundation Educational Institution. I also served, with Josephine Cunnington Edwards, a prolific

New Beginnings

Marjorie E. Johnson (Deceased)

writer of Christian children's stories.

During this time Marjorie continued to try and regain her health. Sadly, on February 23, 1976, Marjorie was laid peacefully to rest in the Laurelbrook cemetery after battling cancer for more than five years.

Indeed this was a sad time for me. I became a single parent of a 13 year old boy, and an eleven year old girl. My faith in my heavenly Father sustained me. He said to me, "Fear not, for I am with you; Be not dismayed, for I am your God. I will strengthen you. I will uphold you with my right hand." Isaiah 41:10. The day of the funeral which was scheduled for 10:00 a.m., the hearse arrived 45 minutes late. We learned that a drunk driver had run the hearse off the road.

After the lunch that had been prepared for us, I sent the children to their church school classes, and I returned to my work and had the prayer meeting service that night.

Several months later, Connie Aikman, a former classmate at Southern Missionary College, wrote a letter telling me that she had an aunt she would like me to meet. Her letter described her aunt. "She loves children and has spent many years in the mission field. At the present time, she is director of nurses at Riverside Hospital in Nashville, Tennessee."

Because I said I would be happy to meet her aunt, Connie made arrangements for her to visit Laurelbrook School. As we visited I

Just a Kentucky Boy

learned that she had been invited to be on the faculty of the school of nursing at Southern Missionary College. From that time on, our friendship grew stronger until Harriet Dinsmore became my beloved wife and a wonderful mother to my children on August 8, 1976. I am thankful for the more than thirty years we have had together.

Harold & Harriet Johnson

After our marriage we received a call from the General Conference asking if we would be interested in foreign mission service. After telling them that we would, we received a call to serve in Malawi, East Africa. I was to be field secretary for the South Lake Field. Before my arrival, the ministerial director for the Southeast Africa Union left, and I was appointed to fill the vacant position. Harriet was to be director of nurses for the Blantyre Clinic. We served in Africa for approximately six years before returning to the States.

During those six years, we enjoyed many visits to the area game parks. Malawi has four national game parks open to the public. Lengwe National Park was the closest to Blantyre—it was about seventy-five minutes away in the Shire Valley in the southern region of the country. It had an attractive camp with chalet accommodations that cost four Kwacha a night, which is about five dollars in U.S. currency. Included in this price were the maid services—cleaning, making the bed, and putting down the mosquito net at night.

Lengwe National Park is a paradise for birders, especially in September and October when large migrant flocks of the Carmine

New Beginnings

Bee-eaters are nesting in the cliffs. On the way down to the park, Blue Cranes could often be seen along the irrigation ditches used for the cane fields. The list of birds could go on and on. With more than 600 birds found in Malawi alone, we saw such varities as the Hamerkop, African Marabou, Glossy Ibis, African Fish Eagle (one of my favorites), African Golden Oriole, Hoopoe, Yellow-billed Hornbill, and Cape Turtle Dove, just to name a few.

The animals were also spectacular. We enjoyed watching the Nyala antelope and the kudu with their large shaped horns. It is a marvel how they can get through the thickets with those large horns. Comfortable blinds had been built at several of the waterholes. We spent some time in them watching Nyala, bushbuck, buffalo, warthogs, kudu, impala, and reed buck—all at close quarters as they were drinking. Of course, monkeys and baboons were almost always present. To see elephants, hippopotami, kudu, and waterbuck plus myriads of bird life, we would also go to Liwonde National Park down by the Shire River.

When Karen and Stephen came on summer vacation, we visited Luangwa National Park in Zambia. While there Stephen jumped out of the car and stepped on a thorn. Unfortunately, the wound became infected, and he had to go through a series of painful treatments to clear up the infection.

At that time Stephen attended Maxwell Adventist Academy in Nairobi, Kenya. After finishing one year there, he returned to the United States to attend Laurelbrook School in Dayton, Tennessee, where he completed his secondary education. Then he attended Southern Adventist College (now Southern Adventist University) where he completed his bachelor's degree in computer science.

Karen enjoyed her stay in Malawi where she finished the eighth grade and the first year of algebra under the tutorship of Lockie Gifford. After completing eighth grade, she returned to Laurelbrook School for high school, after which she attended Southern Adventist College for her nursing training. The children enjoyed being at Laurelbrook, because their grandparents, Walter and Winifred Connell, lived there.

Although visiting with our children and touring Africa were enjoyable, we had come to Africa to work. We arrived in Malawi as they were preparing for the union year-end meetings, which were held before the Trans Africa Division meetings took place. I was immediately initiated into the throes of union meetings. In January we were to begin our ministerial workers' meetings for the union. That meant that I had to make preparation for them and create materials to be used. During the union meetings, it was voted that the division ministerial secretary would hold a major effort in the capitol city of Lilongwe. It was also to be a training effort for the pastors. Before the main effort was to begin, a mini effort was to be held by Pastor Al Long, the division ministerial secretary.

All the plans were laid. In the middle of the mini-evangelistic services, Pastor Long received word that his wife had been taken to the hospital and he needed to be there. He got permission from Pastor Fred Wilson, the union director, to have me finish the meetings. I spent three days copying materials and getting ready for the meetings. Pastor Long left to be with his wife in Zimbabwe, and I completed the mini-evangelistic meetings. Then I launched into the major series. The Lord blessed us with fifty baptisms at the close of the meetings. Later, we had the privilege of baptizing twenty-five more.

After that experience with the evangelistic meeting, I decided that, instead of going through all the red tape of getting permission to hold a major evangelist meeting, I would hold weeklong revivals. I would go into a district and hold at least three different revival meetings in three different places each day. The Lord really blessed with these weeklong meetings.

New Beginnings

There was always plenty of work to do. One Sabbath, even though I planned to be home with my wife and daughter, I ended up having to preach that morning. During the week, I had received a call from the South Lake field director telling me that my associate, who had been scheduled to speak in the large Ndirande Church in Blantyre, would not be needed because the union director planned to speak there. He requested that my associate speak at the nearby Chilangani Church. When I explained the change to my associate, he was very put out.

"If I cannot speak in the Ndirande Church, I will not speak anywhere. I will be in church with my family," he said.

Sure enough, there he was in our home church that morning. After Sabbath School, I told my wife, "I will go to the Chilomoni Church."

When I arrived, I found the field director there. I said, "You may take the service since you are here."

"No," he countered. "I just came to visit. You take the service."

So I had the service, and at the end, I gave a simple call. A man standing in the back immediately came up with several others.

On our way back home, my translator said, "Pastor, did you see the man that came up first? He has been coming to church for several years." My translator continued, "When he came today, he told the elder, 'If there is a call, I will join the church. If there isn't, I will never come back.'"

Hearing that bit of background information left me feeling so weak that I could hardly continue the drive home. Just to think that a soul could have been lost if I had neglected to be there that day and to give a call. My translator and I were in the North Lake field on itinerary, planning to spend the weekend at one of the little churches. When we arrived, the pastor asked me if I would do him a favor and speak that night on witchcraft.

I promised him that I would. Almost immediately, distressing events began to occur. My throat became sore, and I felt dizzy. Thinking that I might be having an attack of malaria, I took some medicine, vitamin C, Benadryl, and lozenges for my sore throat. I went into the little mud hut and lay down on the bed, but the bed seemed to be moving. Later, when I was called to the evening meal, I ate some but could hardly talk. When it was time for the meeting, I stood up to speak, but I could hardly get a word out. Needless to say, throughout this ordeal, I had been praying a lot.

Suddenly, my voice cleared up. I was able to speak clearly and deliver the message of the hour. The devil did not want me to speak on the subject of witchcraft, but the Lord did! He blessed us with several who committed their lives to Him that night. One year later, when I was at the same little church for a baptism, the local pastor explained that he had been forbidden to speak on the subject of witchcraft, but the Lord had been able to use a Kentucky boy as His voice to the people. A large number of the church members had been disfellowshipped because of their involvement with witchcraft.

Having had the privilege of going to Likoma Island in Lake Malawi several times, I made plans to hold a revival meeting there.

"Pastor Johnson, we have a small company meeting on the other end of the island. It is too far for them to come to the meetings. I would like for you to visit them," Pastor Nikosi suggested.

We made an appointment to visit them. I am not sure how far it was from the church and pastor's home to the other end of the island, but walking was the only mode of transportation, and it took at least an hour an a half. When we reached our destination, we met a group of about twenty people.

After meeting with the group, I made the following suggestion to Pastor Nikosi, "Why don't we have a meeting here in the afternoon before the service at the church?"

New Beginnings

All the people eagerly agreed. Therefore, each afternoon we walked to the other end of the island, had a service with them, and returned to the church for an evening meeting. By the time we finished the last meeting at the other end of the island, I had to take my shoes off and walk barefoot because of the blisters on my feet.

Pastor Nikosi carried my shoes and said, "Don't tell the madam that I had to carry your shoes; she might not like it."

As a result of those meetings, we were able to start a second church on Likoma Island. Now, as ships approach the island, the passengers can see a Seventh-day Adventist Church sitting on the hill. Then, as the ship continues on around the island, passengers can see the main church on the other end of the island sitting on another hill.

On my last visit to Likoma Island, I met Gail, a young lady from South Africa. She had just graduated from college and was taking a vacation before starting work. We had a good visit on the way over to the island and back.

"Where are you going next?" I asked her.

"To Lilongwe, the capitol city," she replied.

"I will be going there tomorrow," I told her. "I would be happy to give you a ride."

"I would be happy for that," she replied. "You can pick me up here on the beach in the morning."

My translator and I were spending the night with a government worker. Overhearing Gail's remark, he said, "I have plenty of room in my house. You come with us." She readily agreed to that.

We left early the next morning. As we entered Nkhotakota Game Reserve, we saw a large billboard that read, "Beware of elephants." Pastor D. C. Kasambara, my translator, had never seen a live elephant. As we entered the reserve and started up the mountain, we noticed evidence that an elephant had been there a short time before. Driving

49

Just a Kentucky Boy

along, I was watching for the anthills on the road to avoid hitting one and damaging my car.

"There are the elephants!" Pastor Kasambara announced.

Glancing up, I exclaimed, "Man, those are not elephants! They are lions."

Two male lions were up on a high bank where the road had been cut through a hill. Gail wanted a picture of them but could not get a clear shot because of the tall elephant grass. My telescopic lens would not fit her camera, and I had shot my last slide. While we were sitting there with the car engine still running, one of the lions got up as if to go back into the woods, but we soon realized that it wasn't leaving, instead it crouched closer.

Seeing that, I said, "I think that we had better be going."

As I started to drive off, the lion that had moved closer came right down over the bank. Glancing at my rearview mirror, I could see him following right behind us. The other lion was close beside the car. I was thankful that we were in a closed car.

"Shoot, Gail, shoot!" I urged, but she could not even lift her camera.

Finally, the lions stopped. As we left them behind, I remarked, "I am sure glad that the lion by our side didn't take a swipe at the tire and give us a flat."

"What would you have done if it had?" Gail asked.

"Oh," I replied, "I have a spare in the back, and I would have let you change it."

My teasing did not seem so funny when we found out a few days later that those same lions killed a game warden. A lady and her children also became their victims. The government had to send in national game warden to hunt and kill the lions. (The lions had been molested by men who were poaching for ivory, and the lions were

New Beginnings

turned into man hunters.) This experience brought to mind the words of Daniel to King Darius found in Daniel 6:22 "My God hath sent His angel, and hath shut the lions' mouths, that they have not hurt me."

In February 1983, I was completing my last itinerary before returning to the United States. In one month, I had 115 speaking appointments—quite a busy schedule. After finishing one of my speaking appointments, we stopped at a filling station where we noticed a man getting petrol. As he pulled out, we drove up, but the attendant locked the pump and refused to sell us any petrol.

As we started to pull out, another man called to us and said to my translator, "Don't I know you? I am sure that I know you." After talking for a few minutes, he said, "I heard what that man said. You come with me. I have some petrol at my house that I will give you."

Thus, God provided the petrol we needed, enabling us to keep our next appointment. Later in the week, when we arrived in Mzuzu, we were again in need of fuel to travel to our next appointment down on the lakeshore. When we pulled up to the filling station, we were told that they did not have any petrol.

"Since we cannot get any fuel," I told the pastor with me, "we will need to cancel the appointment. I will call my wife and let her know that all is well."

However, try as I might, I could not get the operator to answer. Returning to the pastor, I reported, "I can't even get the operator to answer."

Just then, I remembered that Jim Goodchild at Lunjika Secondary School had told me that he had someone in Mzuzu getting petrol for him. We found the man five minutes before he closed his store.

When I told him who I was, he immediately told me, "I have the beds for the school and will be taking them down in a few days."

I assured him that I was not there to find out about the beds. I asked if he had been able to get the petrol for Mr. Goodchild, and he said that he had. I explained our plight and asked him if he would let us have the petrol and get more for Mr. Goodchild before he delivered the beds. He agreed to let us have the petrol he had gotten.

After getting the petrol, I again tried to place a call to my wife. The operator answered on the first ring. Again, God had intervened for us so that we could keep our appointments.

We were blessed to serve in the mission field for so many years and witness God's divine guidance and protection; however, it was time for us to move back to the States and let someone else carry on the mission work.

Chapter 7

A Life of Service

Finding a place to serve after returning to the States from the mission field can be a long, drawn-out process. Therefore, I was pleased to be invited to teach in the elementary school in Manchester, Kentucky, soon after our return. After completing one school year, the local Seventh-day Adventist hospital created a chaplaincy position. The position was formed because the pastor was finding it difficult to serve the local church and fill the role of chaplain for the hospital. It was my privilege to be the one to fill the chaplaincy position.

One of the highlights of my service as chaplain at Memorial Hospital occurred just before I retired. I had the privilege of ministering to a retired Navy commander who was a most interesting gentleman. He had graduated from the Naval Academy in 1913 and had retired from the Navy in 1932 with a medical discharge because of a heart condition. He was given about three years to live. Each year he went to Florida for the winter and returned to Kentucky for the summer. He always carried his uniform with him. When he should pass away, he wanted to be buried in it. He passed away in October 1990 in Kentucky.

His nephew attributed his uncle's longevity to the fact that he refused to eat any junk food and he drank a lot of water. He also walked five miles each day. The words of 3 John 2 were true in his life that he would "prosper and be in health."

Just a Kentucky Boy

His nephew asked me to accompany him to Arlington National Cemetery for the interment. When we arrived, the Navy chaplain said, "You do the service. I do not know the man, but you have ministered to him."

"But I do not know the proper protocol for a funeral at Arlington," I protested.

"I will walk you through it," he promised.

Thus it was that I had the privilege of placing this honorable gentleman to rest beside his late wife. Interestingly enough, his uniform was still a perfect fit.

While in Manchester, I had the privilege of attending the annual Adventist Chaplaincy Ministry Convention being held in St. Louis, Missouri. That year the Adventist military chaplains were present. I decided that I wanted to attend one of their meetings, so I left my meeting and went to theirs. After the meeting, I met the late Chaplain (Colonel) Alva Appell, former chief of chaplains for the United States Air Force Auxiliary, Civil Air Patrol. As we were talking, I explained to him that, at one time, I had applied for chaplaincy with the military, but I learned that a hold had been put on all appointments. When the hold was taken off, I was too old to be considered for military chaplaincy.

"You can be too young," he informed me, "but you can't be too old to be a chaplain in the Civil Air Patrol. When you get home, give me a call."

This was my introduction to the Civil Air Patrol Chaplain Service. Chaplain Appell contacted Lieutenant Colonel R. Eugene Figge, Kentucky Wing Chaplain, who in turn contacted Lieutenant Colonel Robert Gray, commander of the London Kentucky Composite Squadron, who accepted me as their chaplain. I was appointed chaplain for the squadron in May 1989 as a captain by the USAF.

A Life of Service

In December 1990 I retired, and we moved to Avon Park, Florida, where we had bought a house. However, my retirement didn't last long, and on January 17, 1991, I started working as chaplain at Walker Memorial Hospital in Avon Park, which was replaced by Florida Hospital Heartland Medical Center in Sebring, Florida. Since retirement, the Lord has blessed me with more than twenty years of service in the chaplaincy.

I also continued working with the military. I transferred to the Highlands County Composite Squadron and served as their chaplain. Later, I became the assistant Group Three Chaplain, and when the Group Three Chaplain retired, I was appointed as his replacement.

Group Three, at that time, consisted of twenty-four squadrons and more than a thousand members. I also served as assistant chaplain to the Florida Wing Chaplain. Later, I was appointed as assistant for recruiting and retention for the South East Region, which consists of Alabama, Florida, Georgia, Mississippi, Puerto Rico, and Tennessee.

I also served as assistant chaplain for recruitment to the chief of chaplain service, United States Air Force Auxiliary Civil Air Patrol at Maxwill AFB in Montgomery, Alabama. During this time, I was the 1,582nd person to have received the Gill Robb Wilson award for having completed the National Staff College at Maxwell Air Force Base in Montgomery, which is the highest training award a senior member can receive. In addition to my work as chaplain at the hospital and with the Civil Air Patrol, I have been appointed by the commander of the Avon Park Air Force Range as volunteer chaplain for the range, serving all branches of services when troops are deployed without a chaplain and there is a need. I also serve as chaplain for B-Battery, 3rd Battalion, 116th FA (HIMARS) of the Florida National Guard in Sebring.

Chapter 8

Overflowing Gratitude

As you journey through life, it is so important to stop and count your blessings. God pours out so many blessings on His children. But we must take the time to look for His providence. As I look back across my life, all I can say is, "Thank you, Lord, for what you have done for 'just a Kentucky boy'!" I received the Distinguished Service Award from Southern Adventist University. The Community Involvement Award from the Adventist Health System, and in 1997, the Civil Air Patrol National Unit Chaplain of the Year.

Our children, Stephen and Karen, are grown-up and married with fine families. And they have given us three wonderful grandchildren.

Son Stephen, Lynda & Ceilidh

Stephen works as a computer specialist with McKee Foods Corporation in Collegedale, Tennessee. He is married to Lynda Magee, who, like Stephen, was born in the mission field. Lynda is an accomplished musician, earning a master's degree from the New England Conservatory in Boston, Massachusetts.

Overflowing Gratitude

Stephen and Lynda are blessed with a daughter, Ceilidh. She is the delight of her grandparents, too.

Karen is married to Patrick Burns, one of her academy classmates. Pat and Karen have two lovely children—John is 15, and Marjorie is 13. They both love living on their farm in Arkansas. Both Pat and Karen are graduates of the nursing department at Southern Adventist University. Pat works in the critical care unit at White River Medical Center in Batesville, Arkansas. Karen also works there part time. They live on a sixty-acre farm near Cushman, Arkansas, on Big "T" Road. They have a herd of cattle and several horses, which the children really enjoy.

Daughter Karen, Pat, John & Marjorie Burns

These are just two of the many blessings our family thanks God for. Life has not always been easy, but we know that God is directing our paths. It is my desire, along with all of God's children, to be loyal to every virtue, true to every friendship, and faithful in the remaining march of God's soldiers that I will be ready, not as a Kentucky boy, but as a son of God, to take my place in the great kingdom of God. I seek to live my life without any doubts but with faith that my heavenly Father will soon say, "Welcome home, my child, where the circle will never be broken."

We invite you to view the complete
selection of titles we publish at:

www.TEACHServices.com

or write or email us your praises,
reactions, or thoughts about this
or any other book we publish at:

TEACH Services, Inc.
P U B L I S H I N G
www.TEACHServices.com
P.O. Box 954
Ringgold, GA 30736

info@TEACHServices.com

Finally, if you are interested in seeing
your own book in print, please contact us at

publishing@teachservices.com.
We would be happy to review your manuscript for free.

www.ingramcontent.com/pod-product-compliance
Lightning Source LLC
Chambersburg PA
CBHW060504110426
42738CB00055B/2616